Madagascar Hissing Cockroach Care

The Complete Guide to Caring for and Keeping Madagascar Hissing Cockroaches as Pets

Pet Care Professionals

Copyright © 2016 Pet Care Professionals

All rights reserved.

Although the author and publisher have made every effort to ensure that the information presented in this book was correct at the present time, the author and publisher do not assume and hereby disclaim any liability to any party for any loss, damage, or disruption caused by errors or omissions, whether such errors or omissions result from negligence, accident, or any other cause.

ISBN 13: 978-1530491896

CONTENTS

Introduction 6

Description 7

    Size 7

    Differences between the Sexes 7

    Natural Habitat 8

    Lifespan 8

    Weight 8

    Diet 8

    Temperament 8

    Skin Shedding 9

Hissing 10

    How is the Hissing Produced? 10

    The Fighting Hiss 10

    The Mating Hiss 10

    The Disturbance Hiss 11

    Communal Hissing 11

Madagascar Hissing Cockroaches as Pets 12

Behavior 12

Handling 12

Permits 13

Recording 13

Housing 14

Housing Multiple Cockroaches 14

Preventing Escape 14

Hiding Spots 15

A Place to Climb 15

Substrate 16

Aspen Shavings 16

Beech Chippings 16

Newspaper and Paper Towels 17

Artificial Grass 17

Temperature 18

Heating the Room 18

Heating Matts 18

Heating Rocks 19

Feeding 20

Dry Food 20

Fruits and Vegetables 20

Water Dish vs. Water Wick 20

Breeding...22

The Act of Mating 22

Live Young...22

Nymphs...22

Mites...24

Where do Mites come from?.............................24

Removing Mites 24

Final Thoughts 25

ABOUT THE AUTHOR 26

INTRODUCTION

The Madagascar hissing cockroach (scientifically named *Gromphadorhina portentosa*) is native only to the island of Madagascar. They are also commonly, and more simply, known as the hissing cockroach or hissers. Madagascar hissing cockroaches are common house hold pets due to their docile temperament and the fact that they are one of the largest species of cockroach. Unlike most cockroaches, the Madagascar hissing cockroach is wingless. As they are unable to fly they have developed an excellent ability to climb and scale a range of different surfaces. Their lack of ability to fly has again allowed this species to develop a tough exoskeleton to protect themselves from predators.

DESCRIPTION

Madagascar hissing cockroaches normally come in a dark reddish brown or black coloring. It is hard to tell the difference between Madagascar hissing cockroaches and other large species of cockroach so it is recommended that you purchase your pet from a certified pet shop or dealer.

Size

Most Madagascar hissing cockroaches will reach a size of anywhere between 1.5 and 3 inches however some have been known to exceed 3 inches in length.

Differences between the Sexes

The male roaches have two large tubercles on the dorsal surface of their prothorax. Many beginner keepers mistakenly believe that these tubercles are the roaches eyes; however the head is actually located underneath this area and is protected by the hard surface of the prothorax. Males also have thicker and hairier antennae than female roaches. Males also sport large horns, which give them an impressive and somewhat unusual appearance.

Female roaches also have tubercles located in the same place as the males. However the females tubercles are noticeably smoother to the touch and much less prominent than the tubercles of the male roach. Female roaches also carry their oothecal (fertilized eggs) internally.

Natural Habitat

The Madagascar hissing cockroach favors forest floors and rotten logs. The main reason for this is that they are able to camouflage themselves among the logs and leaves to protect themselves from predators. Despite their relatively large size, this species of cockroach is capable of hiding within incredibly narrow spaces.

Lifespan

Within the wild the Madagascar hissing cockroach's lifespan is normally between 2 and 5 years. The lifespan for cockroaches in captivity is normally towards the higher end of the average.

Weight

Normally hissing cockroaches weight maxes at about 0.8oz (22.7g)

Diet

The Madagascar hissing cockroach is an omnivore which feeds itself primarily upon vegetables, fallen fruit and other decaying organic matter.

Temperament

Madagascar hissing cockroaches are hardy, docile and are of a relatively small size. They are unable to cause any form of physical harm and are therefore great for beginners.

Skin Shedding

Like many other insects and reptiles the Madagascar hissing cockroach sheds it's skin. Upon shedding their skin the cockroaches normally appear paler than before shedding. If you notice this it is best practice to avoid handling your cockroach as they are more vulnerable to injury during, and just after, the shedding process.

HISSING

The Madagascar hissing cockroach is the only insect species that is known to be able to produce the hissing sound. Other insects are able to produce sounds by rubbing parts of their body together but no insect is capable of producing a hissing noise similar to the Madagascar hissing cockroach.

How is the Hissing Produced?

Hissing cockroaches forcefully expel air through their spiracles (which are tubes that insects use for breathing). The spiracles on a hissing cockroach are found on either side of their abdomen.

The Fighting Hiss

Males hiss periodically while they are fighting over territory. They engage in fights by using their horns and they attempt to push the other cockroach away from the desirable territory. It is very uncommon for a roach to be physically hurt during a fight. While fighting the winning, or more dominant, cockroach will hiss more than the losing cockroach. This suggests that the hissing is a sign of dominance.

The Mating Hiss

Hissing is a common part of the cockroach's mating ritual. Males use their hiss to attract females. As previously mentioned males who are more dominant will tend to hiss more which suggests that female cockroaches will be more attracted to males that issue longer and more dominant hisses. The mating hissing rituals are most commonly performed by males only.

The Disturbance Hiss

The disturbance hiss is made by both male and female cockroaches and it is therefore believe that it is a form of anti-predatory response. However there is little actual evidence to suggest that the hissing is connected to the cockroaches survival. The main reason that it is not completely clear as to why the cockroaches produce the disturbance hiss is that there has been little testing done to prove, or disprove, any theories surrounding the reason for the hiss.

Communal Hissing

It is common for groups of hissing cockroaches, who are housed together, to start hissing in unison. It is completely unknown as to why hissing cockroaches communally hiss but most experts and handlers assume that communal hissing is to establish the hierarchy of dominance within the group of cockroaches.

MADAGASCAR HISSING COCKROACHES AS PETS

As previously mentioned Madagascar hissing cockroaches make very good pets for beginners. They have a docile temperament which allows them to be handled easily. Similarly they have a hardy exoskeleton which protects their body which allows new owners to get used to handling the roaches without fear of harming them.

Behavior

Like the majority of other cockroach species, the Madagascar hissing cockroach is not considered a pest as they do not inhabit human dwellings. As previously mentioned the Madagascar hissing cockroach favors forest floors where they are able to hide themselves beneath leaves, logs and other forest litter. They are more active at night as they use the cover of darkness to safely scavenge for meals.

Handling

As previously mentioned the Madagascar hissing cockroach is a great species for beginner cockroach keepers. Compared to the majority of other cockroach species, the Madagascar hissing cockroach is of a relatively large size which allows for easy handling. They also have a strong exoskeleton which protects the roach from any potential drops which may occur with beginner keepers – however it is best to take care as any drop could still harm the roach despite their hardy bodies. The roach should be gently picked up around the thorax (the hard section behind the head of the roach). Being gentle is important as the cockroaches have sticky pads on their feet and hooks to grip the floor tightly. If the roach is picked up in a sharp jerking motion it can cause the roach harm. When handling your roach you should allow it to roam freely from one of your hands to the other.

Permits

In the USA, some states require cockroach keepers to have a permit before they can keep cockroaches as pets or in breeding colonies. An example of a state which requires a keeper to own a permit is Florida. The University of Florida's Department of Entomology and Nematology, which has a state permit, allows only males to be removed from the laboratory to minimize any chance of a pregnant female being released, or escaping, into the wild. Before purchasing cockroaches it is best to check if there are any rules and regulations surrounding cockroaches in the area where you live.

Recording

It is highly advisable to keep a record throughout your cockroach's life. By regularly noting down weight, length, and feeding patterns you will have a useful resource to help notice any potential problems with your cockroach and to likewise make sure it is in good health.

HOUSING

The Madagascar hissing cockroach is a relatively easy pet to house. Owners should maintain their pet in an area which provides a moist, dark and secluded environment. It is common for laboratories to house large colonies of cockroaches in trash cans. However individual keepers tend to house their cockroaches in glass or clear plastic tanks (normally fish tanks or hamster tanks).

Housing Multiple Cockroaches

In nature the Madagascar hissing cockroach lives in colonies of numerous roaches. This therefore suggests that they are social creatures which again would suggest that there is no issue with housing multiple cockroaches together. If multiple males are housed together they might engage in fights for dominance within the colony but as previously mentioned the losing cockroach is not normally harmed so this should not be an issue.

Preventing Escape

Madagascar hissing cockroaches have specially padded feet which enable them to climb, nearly, any surface. This could be potentially problematic as cockroaches may be able to climb up to the lid of their tank and escape. There are two simple ways to prevent this. The first is to have a securely fitting lid. It is also best practice to have a mesh lid as the mesh makes the cockroaches less able to dislodge the lid. The second method of preventing an escape is to line the first few inches from the top of the tank with petroleum jelly. The petroleum jelly inhibits the cockroaches ability to climb on the tank's surface as is likewise not toxic to the cockroaches health.

Hiding Spots

Madagascar hissing cockroaches like to be able to burrow away from the light. The best method to enable the cockroaches to burrow is down to the choice of substrate. However hiding spots can also be introduced to the tank to give the cockroaches a different option to hide and avoid light. Hiding spots can be made easily from toilette rolls, egg cartons, drift wood or cardboard boxes.

A Place to Climb

As previously mentioned Madagascar hissing cockroaches have specially padded feet that allow them to climb almost all surfaces. Within the tank it is best practice to create additional surfaces for the cockroaches to climb. In laboratories colonies are normally housed in large trash cans which have been divided into sections with cardboard. By dividing the trash can into different sections it gives the cockroaches a vastly greater surface area to climb and explore.

SUBSTRATE

Substrate is defined as the surface, or material, on which an organism lives, grows, or obtains its nourishment. As Madagascar hissing cockroaches are a hardy species there is a wide variety of substrates that can be used to line your cockroaches' tank. It is best to provide a substrate which allows the cockroaches to burrow underneath it to avoid light. Bellow will discuss the benefits of different substrates. It is best practice to vary the substrate used in your tank from time to time to allow the cockroaches to experience change.

Aspen Shavings

Aspen shavings are great for lining the floor of your vivarium. A great bonus is that they collect urine and faeces and can easily be scooped out with a dog or cat litter scoop.

Note: DO NOT use Cedar or Redwood shavings as they are potentially toxic to cockroaches.

Beech Chippings

Beech chippings are cheap and readily available from all reptile stores. They are not as absorbent as Aspen shavings and likewise need to be removed once they are dirtied. However they come in three different grades – small, medium and large. This allows you to choose which grade best suits your cockroach or colony's needs.

Newspaper and Paper Towels

Both newspaper and paper towels are easily obtained and inexpensive. However there is the potential for harmful inks to be present within the paper which make them not ideal for long term use.

Artificial Grass

There are many grades of artificial grass which allows you to choose which best suits your cockroach's needs. Artificial grass is widely available in hardware stores and ironically the cheapest is normally the best when it comes to lining a cockroach tank. The cheapest artificial grass tends to be the most flexible which makes it easier to clean and easier for the cockroach to traverse it. If artificial grass is used it is best practice to have multiple pieces cut to fit the floor of the cockroach tank. This allows for you to rotate the flooring when needed to clean and dry the other pieces. The only downside of artificial grass is that the cockroaches will not be able to burrow underneath it to hide from the light. This problem can be solved by having the cockroach tank in a dark place to begin with but it is still worth considering before using artificial grass as your main substrate.

TEMPERATURE

Madagascar hissing cockroaches are cold-blooded animals and therefore may require an external heat source to maintain proper metabolism. The tank should be placed in a warm location (72 – 76 degrees Fahrenheit) with warmer temperatures leading to an increase in the cockroaches activity and breeding. Cockroaches should not be kept in temperatures below 65 degrees Fahrenheit. They will become inactive and sluggish and long exposure to low temperatures can cause harm or even death. The correct temperature can be achieved in multiple different ways. The three most common ways will be discussed below.

Note: Unless you are planning to breed your cockroaches, or have an especially poor heating arrangement in your home, these precautions and best practices may not be necessary for your individual case.

Heating the Room

Heating the room to between 80 – 85 degrees Fahrenheit is the simplest way to heat your cockroach tank. However this is impractical for long term keepers and is not cost effective.

Heating Matts

If you are housing your cockroaches in an aquarium, or snake vivarium, then it is possible for you to purchase a heating matt to lie underneath your tanks substrate. This allows for the tank to be heated evenly and cost efficiently. Heating matts can be purchased from most pet, or reptile, shops or online.

Heating Rocks

It is possible to purchase hot rocks – which are synthetic rocks which contain a heating element. In our opinion heating rocks are the best practice for heating your cockroach tank. The reason for this is if you place the heating rock on one end of your tank it allows your cockroaches to properly thermo-regulate their body temperatures. Heating rocks are normally used to heat reptile or snake tanks and are therefore easily available in reptile shops.

FEEDING

The Madagascar hissing cockroach is an opportunistic feeder. In their natural habitat their diet will mainly consist of fallen fruit that has landed on the rain forest floor. This fallen fruit provides most of the moisture that the cockroaches need to survive. However they will occasionally drink dew from plants to help sustain their moisture levels. However in captivity the Madagascar hissing cockroach has a wide diet available to it.

Dry Food

Many keepers feed their cockroaches dry food (such as dog food, cat food and fish pellets). The cockroaches are able to survive on a dry food diet as long as water is provided for them to be able to gain moisture.

Fruits and Vegetables

All dry food diets should be supplemented by fruits and vegetables. The range of fruits and vegetables that cockroaches can thrive on is vast: banana, sweet potatoes, grapes, orange slices, carrots, apples and potatoes slices. All moist foods should be fed to your cockroaches in small amounts (about an inch square). This prevents the likelihood of your cockroaches developing high concentrations of fermentation gases which could be harmful to your cockroach.

Water Dish vs. Water Wick

Waster dishes can be provided in your tank to allow your cockroaches to drink. If a water dish is left in a tank for a prolonged period of time it is best to only fill the dish to a shallow level and leave either a sponge or cotton wool in the dish. This is to prevent smaller cockroaches potentially drowning in the dish. However even if all precautions are taken it is still possible for a cockroach to drown in a water dish.

Water wicks are therefore a more desirable option. To create a water wick you need to drill a small hole in the lid of a small container. Fill the container with water and then fill the hole with a wick. Wicks can be made from cotton wool or string. Water wicks absorb the water from the container and allow the cockroaches to drink adequately without the risk of drowning.

BREEDING

As previously mentioned male Madagascar hissing cockroaches hiss to initiate the mating ritual with females. Females on the other hand release an odor to attract males for mating. Both males and females also rub the other sexes antennas to express an interest in mating.

The Act of Mating

Madagascar hissing cockroaches officially commence in the act of mating by rubbing their bodies together. After a short period of time the cockroaches will then turn to connect their bodies together, backside to backside. The males normally initiate this part of the mating process by pressing their stomachs below the females' body as a way of gaining access to their lower bellies. Once connected the act of mating itself normally lasts about half an hour or so.

Live Young

After mating the female "mother-to-be" places the eggs that are fertilized inside of ooethecas, which are a form of container connected to the females body. Ooethecas are normally around an inch in length. It normally takes between 60 and 70 days for the youngsters to hatch. Female Madagascar hissing cockroaches are ovoviviparous – which means that the eggs hatch internally instead of outside their bodies.

Nymphs

Nymph is the technical term given to newly born

cockroaches. Ooethecas usually house between 20 and 60 nymphs. Once these nymphs are born it takes them approximately seven months to become fully mature. They are normally a whitish colour and become steadily more brown as they mature. The mother looks after her nymphs until they have fully matured.

MITES

It is common for your colony, or individual cockroach, to have light-colored creatures crawling on top of the cockroaches body. Similar to how dogs occasionally carry fleas, it is not uncommon for the Madagascar hissing cockroach to carry mites. These mites only live on the roaches body and will not cause the cockroach harm – and likewise are not harmful to humans.

Where do Mites come from?

If your cockroaches have mites it is normally due to their tank not being sanitized properly. Leaving food, shed skin or dead roaches in the tank will attract these mites and likewise give them a medium for survival.

Removing Mites

If your cockroach, or colony, as a mite problem do not worry as they are easily removed. Placing your cockroach in a plastic bag, with a small amount of flour inside the bag, and shaking it gently from side to side dislodges the mites. The mites will then be stuck to the flour inside the bag. Remove the roach and then tie and discard the bag with the mites in it. Use a cotton swab and water, or a gentle water spray, to clean the excess flour off your cockroaches body. Removing mites from a colony is a lengthy process but is not impossible. Clean each roach individually and then place them in a separate container until the whole colony and tank has been cleared of the mite infestation.

FINAL THOUGHTS

Thank you for purchasing our pet care manual on caring for Madagascar Hissing Cockroaches. We hope you have found the information both interesting and informative. We hope that this book has allowed you to make an informed choice on whether owning a Madagascar hissing cockroach suits you and if so we hope that the information will help you to provide the best quality care for your pet cockroach.

We will be publishing multiple other pet care manuals on our author page on Kindle. If you have an interest in exotic and exciting pets then we highly suggest you check out our other work.

Here at Pet Care Professionals we are passionate about providing the best quality information to our customers. We would highly appreciate any feedback, or reviews, you could leave us on our Kindle page to allow us to help create the best possible pet care products available on the market.

ABOUT THE AUTHOR

Here at Pet Care Professionals we are passionate about pet care. As a brand we have a strong idea of what makes up a good pet care book. We consult with multiple experts in each animals field to allow us to create a book filled with cumulative opinions and best practices. The experts we consult range from veterinarians to every day pet keepers who have had years of experience caring for the specific animal each book is on. Our aim, and mission, is to produce the best possible pet care books that are a great value for money.

Madagascar Hissing Cockroach Care

Pet Care Professionals

Printed in Great Britain
by Amazon